Tell Me So I Know

My Questions...Your Answers

Paul Shike

Tell Me So I Know

My Questions...Your Answers

Paul Shike

Graceful Publishing
2015

First Printing: 2015

ISBN   978-0-9963441-0-4

Graceful Publishing
6611 Hillcrest Ave. Suite 427
Dallas, TX 75205
www.gracefulpublishing.com

Contents

Acknowledgments

Many thanks go out to my wonderful family, which instilled the desire for me to know more about their lives, memories and life lessons.

I appreciate the generous support from my friends, many of whom reserved copies of **Tell Me So I Know** in advance of it being published. I am certain you will feel rewarded for your investment as you engage with those special to you.

Thank you Jennifer Lassiter, for taking my work and refining it into a print-ready project. Finding a person with the talent to complete the layout and cover of this book was the final touch needed to make my dream of publishing this book come true.

I would like to thank Chandler Bjork. Chandler interpreted my vision for the cover to create the wonderful artwork for this book. I chose to use elephants for their association with having long memories. The image depicts the beliefs that they provide good luck with their raised trunks and display love by having their trunks wrapped. The outline of the "Tree of Life" is heart-shaped to symbolize the lifetime of love we share with the important people in our life.

Special thanks go out to those who help to further the cause to find a cure for Alzheimer's. The **2015 Alzheimer's Disease Facts and Figures** study published by the Alzheimer's Association (www.alzheimers.org) states that 5.1 million Americans suffer from Alzheimer's, with one in nine people over the age 65 and one in three over the age of 85 affected by this disease.

Preface

I set out with the goal of creating a book to guide you through a number of questions to explore the life of someone special to you. This book also provides a place to record this information.

I hope you will use this book to engage with your parents, grandparents, aunts and uncles, children and other loved ones. Take the time to ask these questions to discover the favorites, life stories, beliefs and memories of those special to you. By sharing this process you will find the bond between each of you strengthened.

The two significant events that inspired me to create this book were the unexpected death of my father, Gene Shike, and witnessing the impact of Alzheimer's on my grandmother and aunt. It did not occur to me that the opportunity to ask them questions about their lives would suddenly end. I find myself wondering daily about the questions I wish I could have asked them. These unanswered questions leave a hollow space in my soul.

I received a call from my sister while I was traveling in Jacksonville, FL. She told me that my father was not feeling well and that the doctors had decided to admit him into the hospital. His kidneys had unexpectedly failed and the doctors said they did not think he had long to live. Shocked to hear this news, I immediately headed to Indiana. He passed eight hours after I first received the call.

Witnessing the impact of Alzheimer's on my grandmother and aunt inspired my writing as well. It seemed as if this horrible disease stole their memories overnight. It is difficult to experience the process of a loved one losing their ability to share their memories.

Many of my conversations with my father were about the latest sporting events. My conversations with my grandmother and aunt did not go much deeper than "how was your week?" I now understand how special it would have been to know their answers to questions such as "What was your favorite memory of me as a child?"

Embrace this book and use this process with the special people in your life. Seize the opportunity to gather this information first hand and strengthen the bonds that you share. Take questions from this book to learn at least one new thing about everyone you know.

It is easy to believe that "tomorrow" will be a good time to ask these questions. Many of the questions in this book I never thought of asking. Many of the questions I did not get around to asking. I certainly wish I knew my father's answers to the questions within this book. Please do not wait! Dad, I wish you could tell me so I know.

How to Begin

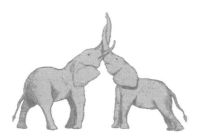

The greatest compliment that was ever paid me was when one asked me

what I thought, and attended to my answer.

~ Henry David Thoreau

Learning of the life experiences and special memories of an important person in your life will be an enriching process. The more we share and know about each other, the greater the opportunity to strengthen our relationships. Before beginning this journey with someone special, be sure to share with them why they are important to you.

The person you are interviewing will usually begin to answer the questions based on their understanding. Do not become bogged down by what exactly a question is asking. You will gain more by listening to the answers, than by debating the correct way to answer a question.

Respect that there are reasons for not wanting to share certain memories. There are no rules stating that the person must answer a question. Conversely, they may want to share their answers to some of the questions with only you. Honor all requests for confidentiality.

Be sure to respect the person's answers. In most cases, there is no right or wrong answer to a question. Avoid challenging them over the details of events. Challenges may lead to a breakdown in the discussion. Be positive and try to keep the discussion moving forward.

For each story, gather as many details as possible. Knowing that you went with your Grandpa Taylor to see the Brooklyn Dodgers vs. the New York Yankees provides a deeper understanding than the mere fact that you went to a baseball game with your grandpa. Details, such as names and places, will help to enhance and preserve the memories.

Be sure to ask "why" as the questions are answered. Discovering your parents' favorite song is great, but knowing why it is their favorite song will be better. Enjoy the additional questions that will certainly arise as you go through the book.

You may not always have the opportunity to sit down together and ask the questions. A great way to work through the book is to ask a few of the questions each time you talk over the phone. Consider scheduling a specific time each week to discuss a few of the questions. As you piece together the information over time, utilize this process to build a stronger relationship.

If you have siblings, consider a group discussion. You may get enhanced answers by asking these questions in a group. The dynamics of the group will help to enrich the discussion.

I do hope that you start sooner rather than later. You never know when you may lose the opportunity to discover this information. My advice is to begin today. Trust from my experience, once you cannot get the answers you will wish that you could go back in time to ask these questions.

Will You Tell Me So I Know?

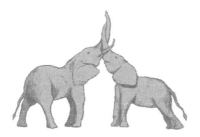

These are the memories and life story of:

_____

From interviews conducted by:

_____

Date(s):

_____

_____

My relationship to this person is:

_____

_____

This person is special to me because:

_____

_____

_____

Let's Get Started

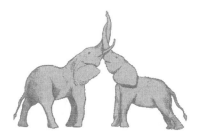

An unexamined life is not worth living.

~ Socrates

This chapter is where the journey begins. You will start by discussing basic information such as your full name, birth date and place of birth. There are questions about early childhood and the things in life that you did not get to choose, such as your parents and siblings.

Be proud of your decision to embark upon this journey. Have fun, laugh, and cherish the memories. The first question is...

What is your full name?

_____

_____

Were you named after anyone? If so, why?

_____

_____

_____

_____

By what name do most people know you?

_____

_____

What other names have you used? Why?

_____

_____

Did you ever wish you were named or called something different?

_____

_____

_____

_____

What are your parents' names? When and where were they born?

_____

_____

_____

_____

What siblings do you have? When and where were they born?

_____

_____

_____

_____

_____

_____

What is the name of your spouse or significant other? When and where were they born?

_____

_____

When were you born? What is your current age?

_____

_____

Where were you born?

_____

_____

What stories do you know about your mother's pregnancy and your birth?

_____

_____

_____

_____

How much did you weigh when you were born?

_____

_____

What color was your hair as a child? Has it changed?

_____

_____

_____

What color are your eyes?

_____

_____

What is your current height?

_____

_____

Have you ever wished you were taller or shorter?

_____

_____

_____

_____

_____

How was your health as an infant?

_____

_____

_____

_____

_____

_____

_____

_____

What do you know about your baby items such as your blanket, stuffed animal, and/ or your first pair of shoes? Do you still have any of these items?

_____

_____

_____

_____

_____

_____

_____

What stories do you know about you as an infant?

_____

_____

_____

_____

_____

_____

_____

_____

Do you have any tattoos? What is the story behind them?

_____

_____

_____

_____

_____

Do you have any birthmarks, moles, scars, dimples or other distinguishing features?

_____

_____

_____

_____

How would you describe yourself today so someone could pick you out in a crowd?

_____

_____

_____

_____

Childhood

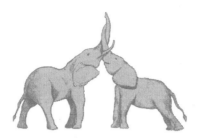

Even a minor event in the life of a child is an event of that child's world and thus

a world event.

~ Gaston Bachelard

Childhood is an amazing time of one's life. As you recall a story, share your perception of the event from your view as a child. Answer the questions with as many details as you can remember. The details will help to improve the understanding of these memories.

What is you first childhood memory?

_____

_____

_____

_____

_____

What is your favorite childhood memory?

_____

_____

_____

_____

_____

How was your health as a child?

_____

_____

_____

_____

What were your thoughts as a child about your parents?

_____

_____

_____

_____

_____

_____

_____

_____

What were your favorite activities with your parents when you were a child?

_____

_____

_____

_____

_____

_____

_____

What was your parent's favorite story to tell about something you said or did?

_____

_____

_____

_____

_____

As a child, how did you get along with your siblings?

_____

_____

_____

_____

Who was your childhood best friend? Are you still friends?

_____

_____

_____

_____

What are some of the activities you did with your best friend?

_____

_____

_____

_____

_____

What did you aspire to be when you grew up?

_____

_____

_____

_____

From your perspective as a child, what did you think about your house and neighborhood? How would you describe it now?

_____

_____

_____

_____

As a child, what are your memories of your pets?

_____

_____

_____

_____

_____

What are some of your favorite birthday memories?

_____

_____

_____

_____

What toys do you remember having? Which one was your favorite?

_____

_____

_____

_____

Did you collect anything as a child? Do you still have any items from the collection?

_____

_____

_____

_____

_____

_____

What were some of your favorite childhood clothing items?

_____

_____

_____

_____

_____

What were your favorite snack foods?

_____

_____

_____

_____

_____

What was your favorite restaurant and food to order?

_____

_____

_____

_____

_____

What was your favorite store to go to as a child? What about it do you remember?

_____

_____

_____

_____

_____

What do remember about your first radio, TV, and record player?

_____

_____

_____

_____

What were your favorite TV shows and cartoons?

_____

_____

_____

_____

What is the first movie you remember watching?

_____

_____

What was your favorite song as a child?

_____

_____

What is the first book you remember reading?

_____

_____

What was your favorite book and why?

_____

_____

_____

_____

Where did you attend elementary and junior high school?

_____

_____

_____

_____

_____

What is your first memory of going to school?

_____

_____

_____

_____

_____

Who were your favorite teachers and why?

_____

_____

_____

_____

What memories do you have about how you got to and from school?

_____

_____

_____

_____

_____

Were you ever in a play? What was it and what was your role?

_____

_____

_____

_____

_____

What activities and sports did you participate in as a child?

_____

_____

_____

_____

What awards did you win as a child?

_____

_____

_____

_____

_____

What do you remember about learning to ride a bike?

_____

_____

_____

_____

_____

What is the first trip or vacation you remember?

_____

_____

_____

_____

What was your most memorable childhood adventure?

_____

_____

_____

_____

_____

What is the most trouble you got into as a child?

_____

_____

_____

_____

_____

What was the most dangerous thing you did as a child?

_____

_____

_____

_____

_____

What was your worst injury as a child?

_____

_____

_____

_____

_____

What weather events do you remember as a child?

_____

_____

_____

_____

_____

What are your memories of major historic events?

_____

_____

_____

_____

_____

What was the most memorable event you attended as a child?

_____

_____

_____

_____

_____

What else would you like to share about your childhood?

_____

_____

_____

_____

_____

_____

_____

_____

_____

_____

_____

High School and College

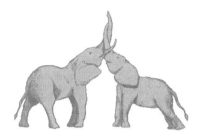

Live as if you were to die tomorrow. Learn as if you were to live forever.

~ Mahatma Gandhi

High school and college are a time in which you become much more independent. You start developing opinions, making decisions, and doing things on your own. Most of us started to drive, experienced our first dates, and established our best friends during this time.

Share the stories of the events that shaped your future. You may have had the best time of your life in high school or college. You may have struggled during this time. The questions in this chapter will help you to explore and share the stories behind these feelings.

Where did you go to high school?

_____

_____

_____

What was your high school mascot?

_____

_____

How many students were in your graduating class?

_____

_____

How would you describe your high school experience?

_____

_____

_____

_____

_____

_____

_____

Did you ever want to go to a different school? Why?

_____

_____

_____

_____

_____

What were your rivals' stereotypes about your school?

_____

_____

_____

_____

Who were your best friends in high school?

_____

_____

_____

_____

_____

How would you describe your peer group?

_____

_____

_____

_____

_____

When not in school, where did you and your friends hang out?

_____

_____

_____

_____

_____

Who from high school do you still consider to be close friends?

_____

_____

_____

_____

_____

Who was the classmate that you most admired? Why?

_____

_____

_____

_____

_____

Who was your nemesis and why?

_____

_____

_____

_____

_____

Did you ever get into a fight? With whom and why?

_____

_____

_____

_____

_____

Is anyone you went to school with famous? If so, how did they gain their fame?

_____

_____

_____

_____

_____

_____

What was your favorite subject and why?

_____

_____

_____

_____

_____

_____

What was your least favorite class and why?

_____

_____

_____

_____

_____

How were your grades?

_____

_____

_____

_____

_____

Who was your favorite teacher and why?

_____

_____

_____

_____

_____

Who were the most influential people in your life during your high school years?

_____

_____

_____

_____

What did you think of your parents while you were in high school?

_____

_____

_____

_____

_____

Did you participate in any sports? If so, what positions did you play and how well did you do?

_____

_____

_____

_____

_____

_____

Were you a cheerleader, on the drill team or in the band?

_____

_____

_____

_____

_____

Did you play an instrument? Do you still play it?

_____

_____

_____

_____

_____

Did you win any special awards?

_____

_____

_____

_____

_____

What are your memories of your school dances?

_____

_____

_____

_____

_____

What songs do you associate with your high school days?

_____

_____

_____

_____

_____

Did you have a car in high school?

_____

_____

_____

_____

Who had the coolest car in school?

_____

_____

_____

_____

What was your dream car in high school?

_____

_____

What did you like to do when you were not at school?

_____

_____

_____

_____

_____

What were your favorite summer activities?

_____

_____

_____

_____

Did you work? If so, what jobs did you have?

_____

_____

_____

_____

Did you babysit? Do you still see that person today?

_____

_____

Do you remember an event you felt was a crisis that you can laugh about now?

_____

_____

_____

_____

_____

What was the most traumatic event you experienced while in high school?

_____

_____

_____

_____

_____

What did you wish you could change about yourself during high school?

_____

_____

_____

_____

Looking back, what two things would you have done differently?

_____

_____

_____

_____

_____

_____

What was the best thing that happened to you while you were in high school?

_____

_____

_____

_____

_____

Did you go to college or trade school? Where did you go and why?

_____

_____

_____

_____

What do you remember about your first day on campus?

_____

_____

_____

_____

_____

What was your major when you started and why did you choose it?

_____

_____

_____

_____

_____

Did you change your major during college? If so, why?

_____

_____

_____

_____

Who was the most influential person in the selection of your major and why?

_____

_____

_____

_____

_____

What was your favorite class?

_____

_____

_____

_____

_____

Who was your most memorable teacher? Why?

_____

_____

_____

_____

How were your grades?

_____

_____

_____

_____

_____

Where did you live during your college days?

_____

_____

_____

_____

Were you in a fraternity or sorority? Which one? What was its reputation?

_____

_____

_____

_____

Did you participate in any college sports? What was your role?

_____

_____

_____

_____

_____

In which non-academic activities did you participate?

_____

_____

_____

_____

What jobs did you have during college?

_____

_____

_____

_____

_____

Were you a fan of your college sports teams? What events stand out in your mind?

_____

_____

_____

_____

_____

Did your sports teams win any championships? What do you remember about them?

_____

_____

_____

_____

_____

Who were your best friends in college? Who do you still talk with and see?

_____

_____

_____

_____

Where was your favorite place to go with your friends? Is it still there?

_____

_____

_____

_____

_____

Who was your favorite local band? When was the last time you saw them?

_____

_____

_____

_____

_____

What songs take you back to your college days?

_____

_____

_____

_____

_____

Who from college do you want to know "what happened to them?"

_____

_____

_____

_____

_____

_____

What are your most memorable college experiences?

_____

_____

_____

_____

_____

_____

_____

_____

What story about your college days do you tell most frequently?

_____

_____

_____

_____

_____

_____

_____

How would you describe your overall college experience?

_____

_____

_____

_____

_____

What are your feelings when you return to the campus of your alma mater?

_____

_____

_____

_____

_____

What do you think about the current status of your college?

_____

_____

_____

_____

_____

_____

Did you go to graduate school? If so, what degrees did you receive?

_____

_____

_____

_____

_____

_____

How do you feel your education prepared you for your career?

_____

_____

_____

_____

If you could go back in time, would you have taken different classes?

_____

_____

_____

_____

_____

What advice would you give to someone starting college today?

_____

_____

_____

_____

_____

_____

_____

_____

_____

_____

_____

Love and Marriage

Once in awhile, right in the middle of an ordinary life, love gives us a fairy tale.

~ Unknown Author

Relationships play a special role in our lives. This chapter covers an area where emotions run the deepest for most people. There are many lessons to learn from the sharing of stories about relationships, love and marriage.

While reminiscing and discussing the questions from this chapter, be sure to look for the twinkle in an eye or the appearance of a smile.

With whom did you have your first crush and why were you attracted to them?

_____

_____

_____

_____

_____

With whom was your first kiss and what do you remember about it?

_____

_____

_____

_____

_____

What do you remember about your first date?

_____

_____

_____

_____

_____

When was the first time you told someone you loved them?

_____

_____

_____

_____

_____

Whom do you consider your first true love? What was special about them?

_____

_____

_____

_____

_____

Based on your life experiences, how would you now describe those feelings of love?

_____

_____

_____

_____

_____

Do you currently know anything about this person?

_____

_____

_____

_____

_____

_____

Who was your worst heartbreak? What happened?

_____

_____

_____

_____

_____

When and where did you meet your spouse?

_____

_____

_____

_____

What do you remember about the first time you met your spouse?

_____

_____

_____

_____

_____

_____

What qualities about this person attracted you to them?

_____

_____

_____

_____

_____

_____

When did you know it was love?

_____

_____

_____

_____

When and where did you get engaged?

_____

_____

_____

_____

What did your parents think about your engagement?

_____

_____

_____

_____

How long did you know each other before getting married?

_____

_____

When did you get married? How old were you and your spouse?

_____

_____

_____

_____

Where did you get married?

_____

_____

_____

_____

Who was in your wedding?

_____

_____

_____

_____

_____

_____

_____

How many people attended your wedding? Did anyone show up unexpectedly?

_____

_____

_____

_____

What are your favorite memories of your wedding day?

_____

_____

_____

_____

_____

_____

Was there any drama on your wedding day?

_____

_____

_____

_____

_____

What are your memories of your wedding reception?

_____

_____

_____

_____

What memories do you have of your Honeymoon? Where did you go?

_____

_____

_____

_____

_____

Do you have any keepsakes from your wedding?

_____

_____

_____

_____

_____

What was your most memorable wedding gift?

_____

_____

_____

_____

Which of your wedding gifts do you still have?

_____

_____

_____

_____

_____

What special memories do you have about any of your anniversaries?

_____

_____

_____

_____

_____

_____

What is your most romantic memory?

_____

_____

_____

_____

What is the most memorable gift you have received from your spouse?

_____

_____

_____

_____

_____

What have been your favorite things to do as a couple?

_____

_____

_____

_____

_____

_____

As a couple, what is "your song"? What memories does it bring back?

_____

_____

_____

_____

What is the most memorable trip or vacation you have taken together?

_____

_____

_____

_____

_____

_____

What is your favorite photo of your love?

_____

_____

_____

_____

What do you feel are the two most important factors for a successful relationship?

_____

_____

_____

_____

Whose relationship do you view as the standard for love? Why?

_____

_____

_____

_____

_____

_____

What is your advice about love?

_____

_____

_____

_____

_____

_____

_____

_____

_____

All in the Family

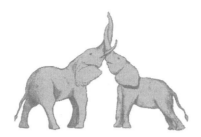

A man travels the world over in search of what he needs, and returns home to find it.

~ George Moore

There is a special bond between the members of a family. Throughout life this bond is the source of many stories and memories. Grandparents, parents, and siblings are blessings in our life. They provide a level of comfort where the only explanation is "we are family."

In many cases, you are the sole person who knows a special story about a family member. By sharing your stories, you provide the opportunity to pass this information on to future generations.

Who do you know from each of the preceding generations of your family?

Great grandparents?

_____

_____

_____

_____

Grandparents?

_____

_____

_____

_____

_____

Do you have any children? What are their names and ages?

_____

_____

_____

_____

What is your favorite memory of each of your children?

_____

_____

_____

_____

_____

_____

_____

_____

_____

What is your favorite memory of your parents?

_____

_____

_____

_____

_____

What is your favorite story about your spouse or significant other?

_____

_____

_____

_____

_____

_____

_____

What is your favorite story about a sibling?

_____

_____

_____

_____

_____

_____

_____

What is your favorite memory of each of your grandparents?

_____

_____

_____

_____

_____

_____

_____

_____

How would you describe the impact that your family has had in your life?

_____

_____

_____

_____

Who would you consider your favorite relative and why?

_____

_____

_____

_____

Who is the most famous member of your family?

_____

_____

_____

_____

_____

_____

What is your favorite story from a family function?

_____

_____

_____

_____

_____

_____

Which of your family traditions are the most important to you?

_____

_____

_____

_____

_____

What are your most cherished family heirlooms and why?

_____

_____

_____

_____

_____

_____

_____

_____

What story would you most like to be passed on to future generations?

_____

_____

_____

_____

_____

_____

_____

_____

Faith

The great act of faith is when a man decides that he is not God.

~ Oliver Wendell Holmes, Jr.

There are different faiths and beliefs. We draw from the power of those beliefs, no matter which faith we choose. Use this chapter to discover the role that faith plays in the life of the person being interviewed.

Listen to the answers and encourage the sharing of these beliefs. Do not make judgments or try to impose your own beliefs on each other during this process. You may decide to use what you share during this chapter as the foundation for in-depth discussions in the future.

How would you describe your beliefs?

_____

_____

_____

_____

When do you remember faith first being introduced into your life?

_____

_____

_____

_____

_____

What person has had the most influence on your spiritual life?

_____

_____

_____

_____

During what events in your life have you called upon your faith to help you?

_____

_____

_____

_____

_____

Have your beliefs ever caused any problems in your life?

_____

_____

_____

_____

_____

Have you ever questioned your faith? Why?

_____

_____

_____

_____

_____

_____

What are the most important benefits you feel your beliefs have had in your life?

_____

_____

_____

_____

_____

_____

_____

_____

What do you think others should know about your beliefs?

_____

_____

_____

_____

_____

_____

_____

_____

What is your advice about faith and a spiritual life?

_____

_____

_____

_____

_____

_____

_____

_____

_____

_____

_____

_____

_____

_____

_____

_____

_____

The Working Life

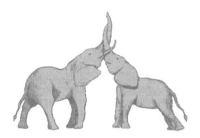

Choose a job you love, and you will never have to work a day in your life.

~ Confucius

For many, the events in this chapter will span the most years of your life. Note how your perception of your jobs has changed over time. You may think your first job was the most difficult job in the world. Now, you may wish that your life were so simple.

The path you have taken has brought many people into your life. There are co-workers who inspired you, while you have inspired others. There are colleagues you have admired, and possibly someone who broke your spirit. All of these people impacted your life and who you are as a person.

Be proud of what you have accomplished. Use your experiences and what you have learned as a reference point for providing and sharing your career advice.

What was your first job?

_____

_____

_____

_____

_____

How did you find your first job?

_____

_____

_____

_____

What jobs have you had during your life?

_____

_____

_____

_____

_____

What has been your favorite job?

_____

_____

_____

_____

_____

Which job did you most dislike?

_____

_____

_____

_____

What job did you want, but did not get?

_____

_____

_____

_____

_____

Which job do you feel provided the most learning experiences?

_____

_____

_____

_____

What is your dream job?

_____

_____

_____

_____

Who was your favorite and least favorite boss?

_____

_____

_____

_____

What person do you feel had the most influence on your career path?

_____

_____

_____

_____

_____

Which co-worker do you feel was the most influential in your career?

_____

_____

_____

_____

_____

Who is the person that you feel you most impacted during your career?

_____

_____

_____

_____

_____

Who is your best friend from work?

_____

_____

_____

_____

What rewards and recognition have you received as a result of your work?

_____

_____

_____

_____

What do you feel is your greatest career accomplishment?

_____

_____

_____

_____

What do you consider the most disappointing event in your career?

_____

_____

_____

_____

_____

What is your advice on balancing your work and home life?

_____

_____

_____

_____

_____

What advice would you give to someone beginning their career?

_____

_____

_____

_____

_____

Money

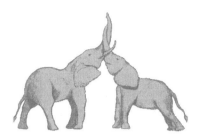

Too many people spend money they earned...to buy things they don't want...to impress

people that they don't like.

~ Will Rogers

Throughout your life money (or the lack of it) has had a direct impact on the decisions you have made, what you have purchased, and what you have experienced. The following questions explore these memories from childhood through the present. Share the advice and insight you have derived from these first-hand experiences.

As a child, what was your perception of your family's financial situation?

_____

_____

_____

_____

_____

Looking back as an adult, how would you now describe your family's financial situation as it was when you were a child?

_____

_____

_____

_____

During your childhood, were there any significant changes in your family's financial situation?

_____

_____

_____

_____

When you were young, where did you keep the money you saved?

_____

_____

_____

_____

_____

What items do you remember buying as a child?

_____

_____

_____

_____

_____

What was your most expensive purchase as a child?

_____

_____

_____

_____

_____

What do you remember about opening your first bank account?

_____

_____

_____

_____

What is the purchase for which you felt the most excited?

_____

_____

_____

_____

What is your most extravagant purchase?

_____

_____

_____

_____

What item that you purchased in the past do you wish you still had?

_____

_____

_____

What purchase do you feel was your greatest waste of money?

_____

_____

_____

_____

What is the most money you have received as a gift? From whom did you receive it?

_____

_____

_____

_____

What is the first work for which you remember getting paid?

_____

_____

_____

_____

How much money did you make in your first job?

_____

_____

_____

Which paycheck are you most proud of?

_____

_____

_____

_____

What was your best investment?

_____

_____

_____

_____

What was your worst investment?

_____

_____

_____

_____

What was your most significant financial crisis?

_____

_____

_____

_____

_____

What would you do differently in regards to managing your money?

_____

_____

_____

_____

_____

What is the largest amount of cash you have had in your possession and why?

_____

_____

_____

_____

_____

What is the largest amount of money you have lost? How did you lose it?

_____

_____

_____

_____

_____

Have you ever been robbed? What happened?

_____

_____

_____

_____

_____

Who in your life has given you the best financial advice? What was it?

_____

_____

_____

_____

_____

How has your financial situation changed during your life?

_____

_____

_____

_____

_____

What is your advice regarding money and finances?

_____

_____

_____

_____

_____

_____

_____

_____

_____

_____

_____

Holidays and Vacations

No man needs a vacation so much as the man who has just had one.

~ Elbert Hubbard

Holidays and vacations are a time to escape from the pressures of everyday life. These are times typically shared with the special people in our life. For many, some of their best memories have been made during holidays and vacations.

Take this opportunity to reminisce and share the special moments and memories from your holidays and vacations.

What is your favorite holiday and why?

_____

_____

_____

_____

_____

What are your first memories of the holidays?

_____

_____

_____

_____

_____

What are your fondest holiday memories as a child?

_____

_____

_____

_____

_____

What are you favorite holiday memories as an adult?

_____

_____

_____

_____

_____

_____

_____

What is the most memorable gift you have received?

_____

_____

_____

What is something you wished for, but never received?

_____

_____

_____

_____

What is the most memorable gift you have given to someone?

_____

_____

_____

_____

What is your favorite holiday picture?

_____

_____

_____

_____

What are your favorite holiday foods and snacks?

_____

_____

_____

_____

What is your favorite holiday outfit?

_____

_____

_____

What special holiday traditions do you remember?

_____

_____

_____

_____

_____

_____

What traditions do you want to be carried on by your family?

_____

_____

_____

_____

_____

What was the first Halloween costume you remember? Which one was your favorite?

_____

_____

_____

_____

What is the first vacation that you can recall ever taking?

_____

_____

_____

_____

_____

What was your favorite vacation?

_____

_____

_____

_____

_____

What is your favorite memory from a vacation?

_____

_____

_____

_____

Where was your favorite vacation picture taken? Who is in it?

_____

_____

_____

_____

Are your vacations spur of the moment or well planned?

_____

_____

_____

_____

What is your best advice on how to pack for a vacation?

_____

_____

_____

_____

Do you have a favorite place where you have vacationed more than once?

_____

_____

_____

_____

_____

Which vacation destination do you want to visit again?

_____

_____

_____

_____

_____

Where would you like to vacation that you haven't been before?

_____

_____

_____

_____

What are your favorite activities while on vacation?

_____

_____

_____

_____

_____

_____

What is the most majestic site you have seen while traveling?

_____

_____

_____

_____

_____

_____

What is the most memorable food you have eaten while on vacation?

_____

_____

_____

_____

_____

What is the most unusual thing to happen to you while on vacation?

_____

_____

_____

_____

_____

Who have you unexpectedly run into while on vacation?

_____

_____

_____

_____

_____

What is your worst experience while on vacation?

_____

_____

_____

_____

_____

What are the states and countries you have visited?

_____

_____

_____

_____

_____

_____

What souvenirs have you acquired while on vacation?

_____

_____

_____

_____

_____

What injuries have you or someone else experienced while vacationing?

_____

_____

_____

_____

_____

Cars and Transportation

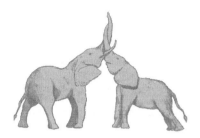

Any customer can have a car painted any colour that he wants so long as it is black.

~ Henry Ford

Cars and transportation are now a large part of most people's lives. Many people are very passionate about the cars they have owned. Share the memories of your parents' cars, your first car and your favorite car.

If you have traveled by air, share your memories of your first experience on an airplane. Think about your experiences with unusual modes of transportation. For some, the use of a horse-drawn wagon has been a part of their everyday life. Enjoy recalling and sharing these memories as you discuss the questions in this chapter.

What are your first memories about cars?

_____

_____

_____

_____

What cars did your family have while you were growing up?

_____

_____

_____

_____

_____

_____

Which family car was your favorite?

_____

_____

_____

What is your favorite color of car?

_____

_____

_____

What was your first car and what did it cost?

_____

_____

_____

What were the makes and models of all the cars you have owned?

_____

_____

_____

_____

Of the cars that you owned, which was your favorite?

_____

_____

_____

_____

Of the cars that you owned, which one did you like least?

_____

_____

_____

What was the most expensive car you have ever purchased?

_____

_____

_____

What was the least expensive car you have ever purchased?

_____

_____

_____

Did you make changes to any of your cars?

_____

_____

_____

Which of your previous cars do you wish you still owned?

_____

_____

What is your dream car?

_____

_____

_____

What are your memories of driving your first motorized vehicle?

_____

_____

_____

_____

_____

How did you learn to drive a car?

_____

_____

_____

_____

_____

When did you get your driver's license?

_____

_____

_____

_____

Why were you given your first ticket?

_____

_____

_____

_____

What are your memories of other tickets you've received? What are the stories behind them?

_____

_____

_____

_____

What is the fastest you have driven a car?

_____

_____

_____

Have you been involved in any serious accidents?

_____

_____

_____

_____

_____

_____

What memories do you have of your longest trip by car?

_____

_____

_____

_____

_____

What are your memories of your friends' cars?

_____

_____

_____

_____

_____

_____

Have you ever owned a motorcycle? If so, what kind?

_____

_____

_____

_____

_____

What do you remember about your first experience flying on a plane?

_____

_____

_____

_____

_____

Is there an event that frightened you while traveling on an aircraft?

_____

_____

_____

_____

_____

Have you ever traveled by private plane?

_____

_____

_____

_____

Have you ever flown in a helicopter?

_____

_____

_____

_____

Have you ever piloted (or wished that you had piloted) a plane, helicopter or hot air balloon?

_____

_____

_____

_____

What is the furthest you have walked or hiked?

_____

_____

_____

_____

_____

What is the furthest you have ridden a bike?

_____

_____

_____

_____

_____

What are your experiences utilizing animals for transportation?

_____

_____

_____

_____

_____

What is your most memorable experience involving animal powered transportation?

_____

_____

_____

_____

_____

How has transportation evolved during your lifetime?

_____

_____

_____

_____

_____

_____

_____

_____

_____

_____

Tell Me Your Favorite

A human being has a natural desire to have more of a good thing than he needs.

~ Mark Twain

We all have our favorites. In this chapter you will share one hundred of your favorite items. Answer the questions as quickly as possible. The first answer that pops into your head is most often your favorite.

Breakfast Food _____

Doughnut _____

Cereal _____

Jelly/Jam _____

Bread _____

Sandwich _____

Cheese _____

Fruit _____

Vegetable _____

Cut of Meat _____

Fish _____

Pizza _____

Salad Dressing _____

Spice _____

Dessert _____

Ice Cream _____

Girl Scout Cookie _____

Cake _____

Perfect Meal _____

Candy _____

Tell Me Your Favorite

Gum _____

Road Trip Snack _____

Soft Drink _____

Coffee _____

Beer _____

Wine _____

Hard Liquor _____

Mixed Drink _____

Fast Food Restaurant _____

Frequently Visited Restaurant _____

Special Occasion Restaurant _____

Color _____

Smell _____

Flower _____

Tree _____

Store _____

Brand You are Most Loyal _____

Piece of Furniture _____

Kitchen Utensil _____

Appliance _____

Tell Me So I Know

Tool _____

Car _____

House _____

City Lived In _____

School _____

Location Visited _____

City Visited _____

Theme Park _____

Beach _____

Lake _____

Park _____

Monument _____

Museum _____

Souvenir _____

Keepsake _____

Collectible _____

Time of Day _____

Day of the Week _____

Weather/Temperature _____

Season _____

Holiday _____

Sport to Play _____

Exercise _____

Board Game _____

Card Game _____

Outdoor Activity _____

Way to Relax _____

Singer _____

Band _____

Concert Attended _____

Song _____

Holiday Song _____

Instrument _____

Actor _____

Actress _____

Comedian _____

Cartoon Character _____

News Anchor _____

President _____

Movie _____

Tell Me So I Know

TV Show _____

Magazine _____

Book _____

Fairytale _____

Broadway Play _____

Sports Star _____

Sports Team _____

Sport to Watch _____

Outfit _____

Blue Jeans _____

Shoes _____

Pajamas _____

Clothing Brand _____

Piece of Jewelry _____

Perfume/Cologne _____

Picture of Yourself _____

Vacation Picture _____

Family Picture _____

Pet _____

Exotic Animal _____

What are three of your least favorite things?

_____

_____

_____

_____

_____

_____

_____

What three things make you the happiest?

_____

_____

_____

_____

_____

_____

_____

154 Choices

Sometimes making a choice has no right or wrong answer or negative outcome. We

simply get to choose between two good things.

~Paul Shike

This chapter has a list of 154 pairs of items. Ask the person you are interviewing to select the item in each pair that is their favorite or best describes them.

To add a fun twist, go through the list and pick the answer you believe the person you are interviewing will select before asking the questions. Do not show the person you are interviewing your selections until after they have made their choices. To keep track of both answers, underline your pick and circle their choice.

Compare how each of you answered the questions. Use the three questions at the end of the chapter to aid your discussion.

Bacon or Sausage

Fried Eggs or Scrambled

Pancakes or Waffles

Toast or Biscuit

White Bread or Wheat Bread

French Fries or Onion Rings

Hamburger or Hot Dog

Ketchup or Mustard

Soup or Salad

Pizza or Spaghetti

Marinara or Alfredo

Cheese Pizza or Supreme

Baked or Fried

Steak or Chicken

Turkey or Ham

Grilled or Sushi

Fresh or Frozen

Sweet or Sour

Spicy or Mild

Sugar or Sweet'N Low®

Apple or Orange

Pie or Cake

Ice Cream Cone or Bowl

Popsicle® or Fudgsicle®

Nuts or Berries

Gum or Mints

Lays® or Pringles®

Cheetos® or Doritos®

Popcorn or Peanuts

Milk Chocolate or Dark Chocolate

Snickers® or Reese's®

Almond Joy® or Mounds®

Cotton Candy or Funnel Cake

Coffee or Tea

Pepsi® or Coke®

Beer or Wine

Can or Bottle

Breakfast or Dinner

Buffet or Table Service

Paper Plates or China

Wash or Dry the Dishes

Cook or Clean

Bath or Shower

Pool or Hot Tub

Inside or Outside

Sun or Shade

Spring or Fall

City or Country

Beach or Mountains

Camp or Hotel

Destination or Journey

Highway or Scenic Route

Sandcastle or Snowman

Fireplace or Campfire

Sink or Swim

Hare or Tortoise

Lover or Fighter

Captain or Mate

Calm or Crazy

Give or Receive

Pitch or Hit

Organized or Messy

Lead or Follow

Patient or Impatient

Focused or ADD

Early or Late

Walk or Run

Stand or Dance

Sit or Pace

Whisper or Scream

Morning or Night

Work or Play

Appointment or Walk-in

Teach or Learn

Draft or Edit

Prepared or Wing It

Smell The Roses or Rush

The Kite or The String

King or Jester

File or Pile

Talk or Listen

Quiet or Loud

Remember or Forget

Hawk or Chicken

Audio or Visual

Diamond or Emerald

Old and Wise or Young and Crazy

Call or Text

Fire or Ice

Love or War

Tough or Meek

Explode or Implode

Create or Destroy

Graceful or Klutz

Rebel or Conform

Bend or Break

Sugarcoat or Blunt

Get Mad or Get Even

Rebuild or Move On

Republican or Democrat

Truth or Dare

Ask For Directions or Get Lost

Salary or Commission

In The Box or Out Of The Box

Future or Past

Hot or Cold

Change or Status Quo

Repair or Replace

Do It Yourself or Hire

Share or Possessive

New or Used

Shop or Buy

Spend or Save

Cash or Credit

Collect or Dispose

Crosswalk or Jaywalk

Window or Isle

Crowds or Solace

Rock or Country

Jazz or Classical

Elvis or The Beatles

Sing or Hum

Guitar or Piano

Waltz or Jitterbug

Slots or Card Games

Football or Basketball

Golf or Miniature Golf

Circus or Fair

Movie or Book

Comedy or Drama

Soap Opera or Game Show

Newspaper or Magazine

Cinderella or Snow White

Mickey or Goofy

Windows® or Mac®

Cat or Dog

Drive or Passenger

Car or Truck

Convertible or Hardtop

Two Door or Four Door

Harley or Honda

Drive or Fly

Glasses or Contacts

Preppy or Grunge

Pants or Shorts

Shoes or Boots

Sweater or Sweatshirt

Sandals or Barefoot

Laces or Loafers

Silver or Gold

Sofa or Recliner

Modern or Antique

Paint or Stain

Carpet or Hardwood Floors

How many of the questions did you answer the same?

_____

_____

Did you think that this number would be higher or lower?

_____

_____

_____

Which answers most surprised you?

_____

_____

_____

_____

_____

_____

_____

_____

_____

_____

I Wish Someone Would Have Told Me

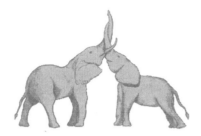

The best time to plant a tree was twenty years ago. The second best time is now.

~ Chinese Proverb

Hindsight is said to be twenty-twenty. There are times you say, "I wish someone would have told me." It is not unusual to feel that with more knowledge, events would have been handled differently or have turned out differently. Use the advice from someone special to avoid the "I wish someone would have told me" moments in the future.

What do you wish someone would have told you about the opposite sex?

_____

_____

_____

_____

_____

What do you wish someone would have told you about dating?

_____

_____

_____

_____

_____

What do you wish someone would have told you about love?

_____

_____

_____

_____

_____

What do you wish someone would have told you about marriage?

_____

_____

_____

_____

_____

What do you wish someone would have told you about in-laws?

_____

_____

_____

_____

What do you wish someone would have told you about children?

_____

_____

_____

_____

_____

What do you wish someone would have told you about siblings?

_____

_____

_____

_____

_____

What do you wish someone would have told you about dealing with idiots?

_____

_____

_____

_____

_____

What do you wish someone would have told you about managing your time?

_____

_____

_____

_____

_____

What do you wish someone would have told you about manners?

_____

_____

_____

_____

What do you wish someone would have told you about school?

_____

_____

_____

_____

What do you wish someone would have told you about work?

_____

_____

_____

_____

What do you wish someone would have told you about money?

_____

_____

_____

_____

What do you wish someone would have told you about cars?

_____

_____

_____

_____

What do you wish someone would have told you about holidays?

_____

_____

_____

_____

What do you wish someone would have told you about your health?

_____

_____

_____

_____

_____

What do you wish someone would have told you about cooking?

_____

_____

_____

_____

_____

What do you wish someone would have told you about life?

_____

_____

_____

_____

_____

Did I Tell You the Story?

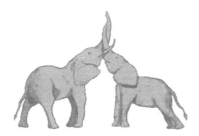

It's not the years in your life that count. It's the life in your years.

~ Abraham Lincoln

We all have stories we love to tell others. Think about the stories that bring back smiles and great memories. There are both firsthand stories from our experiences and stories shared by family members and friends. Recall the stories that you have shared multiple times during your life.

Document what you learn about these stories. Over time, it may become difficult to recall these details from your memory.

What is your favorite story about your childhood?

_____

_____

_____

_____

_____

_____

_____

What is your favorite story about you?

_____

_____

_____

_____

_____

_____

_____

What is your favorite story that you most often tell others?

_____

_____

_____

_____

_____

_____

_____

What is the story you tell that gets the most laughs?

_____

_____

_____

_____

_____

_____

_____

What is a story you remember telling at your high school reunion?

_____

_____

_____

_____

_____

_____

_____

_____

What is your favorite story about the person interviewing you?

_____

_____

_____

_____

_____

_____

_____

_____

What was your closest brush with death?

_____

_____

_____

_____

_____

_____

_____

_____

What is your favorite vacation story?

_____

_____

_____

_____

_____

_____

_____

_____

What is your favorite story about you winning something?

_____

_____

_____

_____

_____

_____

_____

What is your favorite story about a friend?

_____

_____

_____

_____

_____

_____

_____

What is your favorite story about an event you attended?

_____

_____

_____

_____

_____

_____

_____

What is the story behind you learning one of life's lessons?

_____

_____

_____

_____

_____

_____

_____

The Future and the Past

Life is divided into three terms -that which was, which is, and which will be. Let

us learn from the past to profit by the present, and from the present to live better in

the future.

~ William Wordsworth

Life has a past, present and future. How different would your life be if you could go back and change the past or see into the future? Who from your past do you wish you could spend one more day with? If this were possible, what would you want to do with them?

Use this opportunity to explore your past and your thoughts about the future.

What is one thing that you hope to achieve that you have not yet accomplished?

_____

_____

_____

_____

_____

If you could see into the future, what would you want to know?

_____

_____

_____

_____

_____

If you could see into the future, what would you not want to know?

_____

_____

_____

_____

_____

What are two things you would like to happen in the future?

_____

_____

_____

_____

_____

What are your thoughts on what the future has in store for you?

_____

_____

_____

_____

_____

_____

What is the decision you most regret making during your lifetime?

_____

_____

_____

_____

_____

If you could change your past, what are two things that you would do differently?

_____

_____

_____

_____

_____

How would these changes impact your life?

_____

_____

_____

_____

_____

What was the best day of your life?

_____

_____

_____

_____

_____

Who would you like to meet during your lifetime?

_____

_____

_____

_____

Who have you not forgiven for something they have done? Do you wish you had?

_____

_____

_____

_____

How do you want to be remembered?

_____

_____

_____

_____

If you could bring two people back and spend a day with them, who would they be? What would you do with them?

_____

_____

_____

_____

_____

_____

_____

_____

_____

_____

For what five things are you the most grateful?

1._____

_____

_____

_____

_____

2._____

_____

_____

_____

_____

3._____

_____

_____

_____

_____

4._____

_____

_____

_____

_____

5._____

_____

_____

_____

_____

Technology and Science

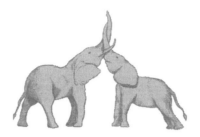

It is strange that only extraordinary men make the discoveries, which later appear so

easy and simple.

~Georg C. Lichtenberg

Think of the things that have changed during your life. The list may include items such as automobiles, electricity in the home, indoor plumbing, radios, telephones, color TV, laptop computers and/or recent developments like the iPhone.

Explore the stories associated with the most memorable changes in technology and science you have experienced. Enjoy recalling your feelings and reactions the first time you were introduced to a new technology.

We have learned throughout life that the only constant in the world is change.

As a child, what were the new technology items you remember your family acquiring?

_____

_____

_____

_____

_____

_____

_____

What were the most memorable technological and scientific discoveries you remember as a child?

_____

_____

_____

_____

_____

_____

_____

Which technology items do you feel have most significantly impacted your life?

_____

_____

_____

_____

_____

_____

_____

Which technology items do you feel have had the most impact on the world?

_____

_____

_____

_____

_____

_____

_____

What is one technology item you purchased that you felt was a waste of money?

_____

_____

_____

_____

_____

_____

_____

What are two technology items you have wanted, but never acquired?

_____

_____

_____

_____

_____

_____

_____

What do you feel have been the most memorable medical innovations during your lifetime?

_____

_____

_____

_____

_____

_____

_____

What advancements in medical technology have been critical in helping you or someone close to you?

_____

_____

_____

_____

_____

_____

_____

_____

Service to our Country

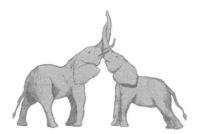

The nation which forgets its defenders will be itself forgotten.

~ Calvin Coolidge

Service to our country is a noble act and an important chapter in a person's life. There are those that volunteer and others that have been drafted to serve our country. We need to recognize these brave men and women as heroes.

Experiences vary from serving our country, and each person's life may have been affected differently. There are those that incurred life-changing injuries. Some may not want to discuss the horrors they experienced. For many, this is the most rewarding time of their life.

There are those who make a career of serving their country. Others see it as a brief stop along the road of life.

Use this chapter to learn about the hero within the person with whom you are sharing this process.

Who was the inspiration for your decision to join the military?

_____

_____

_____

How long did you serve?

_____

_____

_____

What is the highest rank you achieved?

_____

_____

_____

In which branch did you serve?

_____

_____

_____

Why did you select the branch in which you served?

_____

_____

To which division, wing, ship or specialty group where you assigned?

_____

_____

_____

What is the history of this group? What is their motto?

_____

_____

_____

What are your memories of boot camp or basic training?

_____

_____

_____

_____

What were the specialized trainings and/or schools you attended?

_____

_____

_____

Which training was the most difficult?

_____

_____

_____

_____

_____

Which training was the one you enjoyed the most?

_____

_____

_____

_____

Where have you been stationed?

_____

_____

_____

_____

On your deployments, where were you sent and how long were you deployed?

_____

_____

_____

_____

_____

What do you remember about your deployments?

_____

_____

_____

_____

What medals and accommodations have you received?

_____

_____

_____

_____

_____

With whom from your military career do you continue to stay in contact?

_____

_____

_____

_____

What experiences from the military do you still apply to your everyday life?

_____

_____

_____

_____

What is your advice about joining the military?

_____

_____

_____

_____

_____